FINNISH CHILDREN'S BOOK

YOUR CHILD'S FIRST 30 WORDS

ILLUSTRATED BY:
FEDERICO BONIFACINI

ROAN WHITE

TEACH YOUR CHILDREN ALL THE NEW WORDS THEY NEED TO LEARN EARLY WITH THIS BOOK.

INCLUDING 30 OF THE MOST USEFUL, FUN, HAPPY WORDS, THIS COLORFUL, GORGEOUSLY ILLUSTRATED BOOK WILL BREATHE HAPPINESS AND PASSION FOR LANGUAGE INTO YOUR CHILD'S LIFE.

FROM MOM TO APPLE TO DOG TO RAIN TO PUDDLE, THIS BOOK BRINGS ALL THESE WORDS INTO YOUR KIDS LIFE THROUGH GORGEOUS ILLUSTRATIONS.

ALL VOCABULARY IS IN FINNISH.

ÄITI

ISÄ

OMENAPIIRAKKA

SUKLAA

JOGURTTI

PANNUKAKKU

HALAUS

LINTU

VESI

TÄHDET

KOIRA

KISSA

KIRJA

NUKKE

BANAANI

MANSIKKA

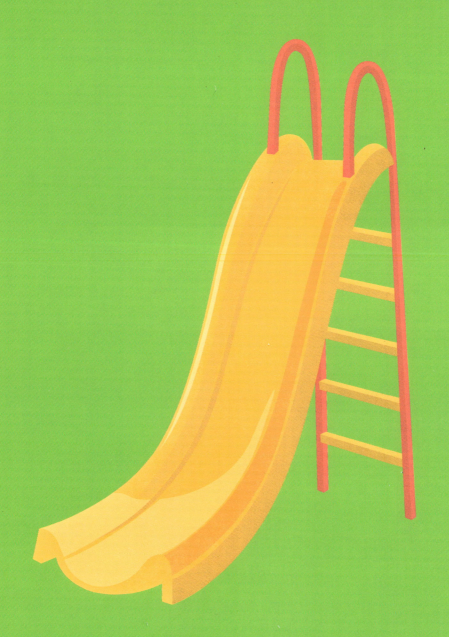

LIUKUMÄKI

KANA

LÄTÄKKÖ

JÄÄKAAPPI

TIETOKONE

SADE

SATEENKAARI

SUUKKO

AUTO

TALO

LENTOKONE

KUORMA-AUTO

VÄRILIITU

HIEKKA